AF490510

"You are braver than you believe,smarter than you seem, and stronger than you think."

-    Winnie-the-Pooh (A.A. Milne)

Foreword

Growing up, my mom, and others like my mom, played an integral part in my life. Unfortunately, my mother was taken away far too soon. I sometimes fear the same will happen to my girls - that I will not get a chance to impart some important knowledge, or pearls, as it were, that will make their lives even easier. I decided to write some down for them and maybe even for their daughters (children). These are things I wish I could have had in my hands as I got older. There are also things I've learned or discovered along my journey, that unfortunately I had to learn on my own. Perhaps some of the bumps and bruises could have been avoided if I'd had my mother's wisdom. May she rest in heaven peacefully.

When I Became a Mom

WHEN I BECAME A MOM

When I found out I was pregnant, I swore I'd be the best mother I could be. I'd follow in the footsteps of my own mother, her mother and her mother's mother.When each of you were born, I promised to protect you like a "mama bear," keeping you free from all the harm and evils of the world. I committed to raising you to be strong, yet sensitive, independent, yet loving, young women; trying to constantly impart knowledge you could use later while still allowing you to be your unique selves– a difficult balance to attain. I have been blessed with two lovely daughters (and a niece who is like a daughter) who should know I'd fight anyone and anything for them and take on the burdens of the world for them if I could.

As I watched you blossom into teenagers and young adults, I have been so extremely proud of your progress. I know you eventually need to find your own way though. I must constantly fight off my "mama bear" instincts to shield you from bad decisions, bad people, and the troubles of the world. There are still a lot of things I want and need to share as you continue your journey to womanhood. Many of these are the things I wish my mother (and/or my father, or even my mother figures) would have shared with me to help me avoid many of the speed bumps in life.

There are also a lot of things they shared that I honestly could not appreciate until I was grown with my own child- rearing responsibilities. I sat up one night and decided I would put some of these pearls of wisdom to paper so no matter what, you will always have my thoughts with you and maybe even share them with your children one day.

I read a poem written by my mother in 1972. I was only 5 years old at the time! My mother was an excellent writer and poet who liked creating songs, short stories, and poems. I am including this in my book as homage to her and to help you better understand me and my upbringing.

My mother could've chosen a different life, after all she was smart, educated and as you will see from her poetry, skilled in the use of words. I wish I'd had more time with her to get to know her in an adult-mother relationship, as a grandmother and as a "friend" in my adult years. I wish you would've had her in your lives as well. I know from watching her mother

(Grandmommy), and her sisters, she would've been one of those grandmas or nanas who was extremely close to her grandkids. My sister (Karma) and I joke all the time about how if our parents had lived long enough to enjoy the grandparent years, our children probably would have preferred them over us (lol).

My mother, Sheri Sandela Richardson Ede, was a talented writer. It wasn't until many years after her death that I really understood how deep her poems, stories and songs were and how she poured out her life in those words. This one is entitled, "To Dream Your Life Away." (12/13/72)

"One of the hardest lessons I intend to teach our two little girls (who will most likely turn out to be wives and mommies) is that of accepting the present for what it's worth and using dreams of the future as much as possible as a step towards real plans and actions. I will say avoid "the impossible dream"! Here stands one mother who will draw the line on make-believe and feed a little of life's bitter truths to her children at an early age so that the taste will not come to them all at once or as a surprise. They will accept the taste as a part of life and the sweet will seem sweeter for having known it."

If I can be half the mother she was and a percentage of the mother her mother was, then I will have done good!

The Pearls (of wisdom)

THE PEARLS

So here are some sayings and "pearls of wisdom" I want to make sure you have in life. There may even be familiar things you have heard me say to you already. I'm sure as you grow into young women and one day become moms yourself, you will add more to the list.

Be nice to others, because what you put out in the world is what you get back.

"Be the good you want to see in the world."

- Ghandi

Your parents aren't too old to remember their first loves, heartbreaks, and other defining moments. We can impart some knowledge in these areas.

Love is love no matter your age.

"Love is patient, love is kind. It does not envy, it does not boast, it is not proud. It is not rude, it is not self-seeking, it is not easily angered, it keeps no record of wrongs. **Love** does not delight in evil but rejoices with the truth."

- 1 Corinthians 13:1

Treat your family well. You never know when you may lose them. Regret is a horrible, horrible thing. "These 3 words, sweet and simple..." by Stevie Wonder rang so true to me when Ammari passed away. Listen to the song some time if you can. You know how much I love Stevie! I got that from my mom who played his music regularly, especially during Saturday morning cleaning time. She even said she'd sent him some of her poetry and songs.

Tell those you love how you feel while you can. Give them their "flowers" while they can still smell them.

"The way to love anything is to realize that it may be lost."

- G.K. Chesterton

Your sister will and should always love you back and vice-versa. There will come a day when you need to lean on each other, so be good to one another and constantly forgive, even when you don't really want to do so.

I am my sister's keeper.

"Sister is probably the most competitive relationship within the family, but once the sisters are grown, it becomes the strongest relationship."

- Margaret Mead

Hard work usually pays off. Developing good habits early will save you time and aggravation later.

Short term pain, long term gain.

"Hard work beats talent when talent doesn't work hard."

- Tim Notke

Boys (men) have not changed since your parents were teens. Believe me when I say:

The game is still the game.

"The thing that hath been, it is that which shall be; and that which is done is that which shall be done: and there is no new thing under the sun."

- Solomon

If you have one true friend in this world, you are blessed. Nurture and cultivate that friendship and you will have a friend for life.

Sow seeds of friendship and reap the reward.

"As you grow older, you realize it becomes less important to have more friends and more important to have real ones."

- Ziad K. Abdelnour

Respect your elders as it reflects *your* character and up-bringing. It is the best way to pay homage to those who are no longer here. Teach this to your children too.

Raise a child with discipline and respect.

"Direct your children onto the right path, and when they are older, they will not leave it."

- Proverbs 22:6, NLT

Strive for greatness. You will encounter obstacles along the way but keep your eye on the prize. I know you can hear me saying this as I stole it from my father.

Do great things!

"Be not afraid of greatness. Some are born great, some achieve greatness, and others have greatness thrust upon them."

- William Shakespeare

No man worth his salt wants a messy, nasty woman.

Cleanliness is next to Godliness.

"Neatness and cleanliness is not a function of how rich or poor you are but that of mentality and principle."

- Ikechukwu Izuakor

Learn all you can from your parents because they will not live forever. Learn how to cook, clean, change a tire and thread a needle.

Life is short.

"The trouble is, you think you have time."

- Buddha

Learn to forgive others (and family), especially those who you know did the best with what they had to give. Forgive them for your sake, *not* theirs.

Forgiveness frees the soul.

"Forgive others, not because they deserve forgiveness, but because YOU deserve peace."

- Jonathan Lockwood Huie

"To forgive is to set a prisoner free and discover that the prisoner was you."

- Lewis B. Smedes

Try not to hold grudges against your parents, particularly if they were not there for you like you may have preferred. Parents are human and make mistakes too.

Let it go…

"To understand somebody as a human being, I think, is about as close to real forgiveness as one can get."

- David Small

"Sometimes letting things go is an act of far greater power than defending or hanging on."

- Eckhart Tolle

It is okay to be strong, independent, yet vulnerable. So, don't be afraid to let someone into your heart or take care of you.

You may get hurt, but you also may find the love of your life. You will not know which until you try.

"'Tis better to have loved and lost, than never to have loved at all."

- Alfred Lord Tennyson

Since we all must "make ends meet" through our jobs/careers, do something you love so your days are not filled with forced work. Try to work in your passion, or if there is more than one passion, pick one to make into a career.

Do what you love.

"Do what you love, and the money will follow."

- Marsha Sinetar

Some people will only be in your life for a season. It's okay. A lesson is learned from every encounter.

Not everyone is meant to be in your life forever.

"People come into your life for a reason, a season, or a lifetime. When you figure out which it is, you know exactly what to do…"

- Unknown

Keep God first. Lean on Him for support and guidance. There will be times when you will question your faith in God. He understands you might need time to regain your faith.

Your belief in a higher power will get you through the hard times.

"Faith isn't a feeling. It's a choice to trust God even when the road ahead seems uncertain."

- Toby McKeehan

Find a husband who is equally yoked. A Godly or spiritual man with morals, work ethic and dreams like your own. One who is not afraid to cry or let you shine and succeed.

There are still good men in the world, it may just take little while to find him.

"Don't team up with those who are unbelievers. How can righteousness be a partner with wickedness? How can light live with darkness?"

- 2 Corinthians 6:14, NLT

"Your soul is attracted to people the same way flowers are attracted to the sun. Surround yourself only with those who want to see you grow."

- Pavana

Get an education. It's a competitive world out there. Education will always be important. Be a continuous learner. An education does not always come from a degree, but educate yourself, nonetheless.

Education is a journey, not always just a destination.

"Once you stop learning, you start dying."

- Albert Einstein

"Work harder on yourself than you do on your job. If you work hard on your job, you can make a living. If you work hard on yourself, you can make a fortune... Income seldom exceeds personal development."

- Jim Rohn

Dream big and go for it! Don't be afraid to try something new because you can always change course later, especially while you are young.

Course corrections are okay if you get something out of it.

"Your life does not get better by chance. It gets better by change."

- Jim Rohn

"Sometimes life throws us a curve. Only later do we realize it was a course correction."

- Tessa Cason

Do not be fooled by new shiny things. Make sure it, or they, are authentic. You may really want to be with someone or do something that is *only* good for the moment.

Everything that is good <u>to</u> you is not good <u>for</u> you.

"All that glitters is not gold."

- William Shakespeare

Learn how to use a needle and thread, iron, fix a leaky sink and use basic tools. It's okay to ask for help, but it is also a good thing to know the basics yourself.

Being self-sufficient is not a bad thing.

"There is no limit to what we, as women, can accomplish."

- Michelle Obama

"Only the self-sufficient stand-alone – most people follow the crowd and imitate."

- Bruce Lee

Stand up for what you believe in and exercise your right to vote. Voting was not always an option for women or African Americans.

Every vote does count.

"You don't get to complain, if you don't vote!"

- Charles Ede

Do not forget your heritage and teach it to your own children. There are so many things that will not be found in the school text books and so many historical points that if not learned will be repeated.

Know your history so you can plan your future.

"Those who don't know history are doomed to repeat it."

- Edmund Burke

Do not live in debt. You may ultimately have some level of debt but strive to *not* live off credit cards. Financial freedom is important. Don't live to work, work to live.

Pay yourself first!

"The rich rule over the poor, and the borrower is slave to the lender."

- Proverbs 22:7 (NIV)

Take care of your mind and body. Peace and harmony
in life are wonderful things and ultimately affect your
health.

Your body is your temple. Treat it as such.

"Take care of your body. It's the only place you have to
live."

- Jim Rohn

Don't be afraid to just be **you**. Spend some time discovering the beautiful person you are and embrace her!

There is no one else in the world quite like YOU. And that's okay!

"Never apologize for being yourself."

\- Paulo Coelho

"Always be a first-rate version of yourself and not a second-rate version of someone else."

\- Judy Garland

Give to those less fortunate. Realize there are people who may not have had the same opportunities and they are important in this world too.

We are all God's children, and your act of kindness may change or even save a life.

"In a world where you can be anything, be kind."

- Jennifer Dukes Lee

Surround yourself with like-minded people. Negative people or those who create drama/problems in your life, should not be in your circle of acquaintances.

To change your life, often means changing your relationships.

"The more you feed your mind with positive thoughts, the more you can attract great things into your life."

- Roy T. Bennett

Do not put off until tomorrow what can be done today.

Do it now.

"Do it now. Sometimes later becomes never."

- Victoria Holt

"A year from now, you will wish you had started today."

- Karen Lamb

Don't fall in love with only "potential."

While potential is great, it may mean there's no actual action.

"I like to think of ideas as potential energy. They're really wonderful, but nothing will happen until we risk putting them into action."

- Mae Jemison

It's okay to be frugal and not keep up with others.

Things do not define you. YOU define you.

"A penny saved is a penny earned."

- Benjamin Franklin

"He who buys what he does not need steals from himself."

- Swedish Proverb

Sometimes things are beyond your control.

It is what it is (sometimes).

"Life is 10% what happens to you and 90% how you reactto it.

- Charles R. Swindoll

"God, grant me the Serenity to Accept the things I cannot change, Courage to change the things I can, and Wisdom to know the difference."

- Reinhold Niebuhr

It's often hard to maintain the discipline and stamina needed to reach your goals.

If you stay the course, you will receive the fruits of your labor.

"Discipline is choosing between what you want **now** and want you want **most**."

- Abraham Lincoln

The mind is a powerful thing. You can tap into your own blessing and potential by having the right mindset.

Manifest what you want in your life.

"What you _think_, you _become_. What you _feel_, you _attract_. What you _imagine_, you _create_."

- Buddha

"If you believe it will work out, you'll see opportunities. If you believe it won't, you will see obstacles."

- Wayne Dyer

We want to see the good in people most of the time. If someone is not what you thought, that's okay.

Don't get fooled multiple times by the same actions.

"When someone shows you who they are, believe them the first time."

- Maya Angelou

Making a living is important. You both have taught me you also must be valued and respected there too.

Work to live and don't live to work.

"Life is short…work where you're continuously accepted, encouraged, inspired, empowered, and valued."

- Ty Howard

It's okay to change course as many times as you like. Change can be scary, but you don't get results without it.

Change can be a good thing sometimes.

"One reason people resist change is because they focus on what they have to give up, instead of what they have to gain."

- Rick Godwin

"If you don't like how things are, change it! You're not a tree."

- Jim Rohn

Remember though when you are making a change that without direction, you may end up in a place you hadn't intended.

It's up to you to choose the direction and actions necessary to get to where you want to be.

"Direction, not intention determines your destination."

- Andy Stanley

"In all thy ways acknowledge him, and he shall direct thy paths."

- Proverbs 3:6

"Your own ears will hear him. Right behind you a voice will say, 'This is the way you should go,' whether to the right or to the left."

- Isaiah 30:21 (NLT)

Surround yourself with like-minded people. They will help uplift you and vice versa. As you grow, unfortunately some people will not fit into your plan anymore. Remember the "grabs in the bucket" story.

Sometimes to change your circumstances, you must change your relationships and circle of friends.

"Anything is possible when you have the right people there to support you."

- Misty Copeland

"Surround yourself with people that push you to do better. No drama or negativity. Just higher goals and higher motivation. Good times and positive energy. No jealousy or hate. Simply bringing out the absolute best in each other."

- Warren Buffet

Happiness is a state of mind. You must find it within yourself.

You are the only responsible and in control of your happiness.

"If you always think your happiness is somewhere else, it'll never be where you are."

- David Wolfe

"Happiness is not the absence of problems, it's the ability to deal with them."

- Steve Maroboli

It's often hard to let go of anger and frustration, especially when it comes to relationships with those you love or when plans don't work like you want.

Try to let go. And let God.

"Every time you get upset at something, ask yourself if you were to die tomorrow, was it worth wasting your time being angry."

- Robert Tew

"If you focus on the hurt, you will continue to suffer. If you focus on the lesson, you will continue to grow."

- Buddha

Start building good habits, even when it's hard. They say it takes at least 21 days to form a good habit.

Continuing bad habits and expecting things to change is a futile mission.

"People do not decide their futures, they decide their habits and their habits decide their futures."

- F.M. Alexander

No matter what you ultimately decide to believe, or the name you give, there is a power that is greater than us all.

53

Your relationship with God, the Universe, or the Spiritual is your own personal journey.

"God is not a Christian. God accepts as pleasing those who live by the best lights available to them that they can discern. All truth, all sense of beauty, all awareness of goodness has one source, God, who is not confined to one place, time or people."

- Desmond Tutu

Sometimes the going will get tough and you'll want to quit. Unfortunately, the world will keep turning.

Time is going to pass regardless, so it is up to you to decide how you will spend it.

"We either make ourselves miserable, or we make ourselves strong. The amount of work is the same."

- Carlos Castaneda

Being called sensitive or emotional was always seen as being weak as I was growing up. I wish I had shown more of this side of myself to you both.

Be who you really are and don't apologize for it!

"Never apologize for being sensitive or emotional. It's a sign that you have a big heart and that you aren't afraid to let others see it. Showing your emotions is a sign of strength."

- Brigitte Nicole

My loves, I began by talking about how short life can be. But I look forward to sharing more nuggets and pearls of wisdom with you (and your kids), God willing. I wish you nothing but a long, happy, and prosperous life, filled with all the joy and love your heartcan hold.

I love you to the moon and back!

"Believe in yourself and all that you are. Know that there is something inside you that is greater than any obstacle."

- Christian D. Larson

<u>DEDICATIONS</u>

I dedicate this book to my mother! I also want to acknowledge my aunts, sisters - Karma and Ammari, sistah-friends, mother-figures and others who have played a role in making me the woman I am today. I love all of you!!!

Notes and Reflections of Your Own